PIONEERS AT SEA

by Alex Hall

Minneapolis, Minnesota

Credits

Images are courtesy of Shutterstock.com. With thanks to Getty Images, Thinkstock Photo, and iStockphoto. Recurring images – Elena Pimukova, Svetolk, Dancake. Cover – Ravelios, Regien Paassen. 4–5 – Alvov, Jenna Aloia Photography. 6–7 – Ivan Marc. 8–9 – Sharon Mollerus, CC BY 2.0 <https://creativecommons.org/licenses/by/2.0>, via Wikimedia Commons, Riptaid. 10–11 – beibaoke, Kosov vladimir 09071967, CC BY-SA 4.0 <https://creativecommons.org/licenses/by-sa/4.0>, via Wikimedia Commons. 12–13 – Jaime Grech Santos. 14–15 – 24K-Production, Prachaya Roekdeethaweesab. 16–17 – svic. 18 – Hirarchivum Press. 20–21 – Janaka Dharmasena. 22–23 – Olga Popova. 24–25 – Leo Wehrli, CC BY-SA 4.0 <https://creativecommons.org/licenses/by-sa/4.0>, via Wikimedia Commons. 28–29 – Mongkolchon Akesin, blue-sea.cz, Osipov Art. 30 – VladyslaV Travel photo.

Bearport Publishing Company Product Development Team

Publisher: Jen Jenson; Director of Product Development: Spencer Brinker; Managing Editor: Allison Juda; Editor: Cole Nelson; Associate Editor: Naomi Reich; Associate Editor: Tiana Tran; Art Director: Colin O'Dea; Designer: Kim Jones; Designer: Kayla Eggert; Product Development Specialist: Owen Hamlin

Library of Congress Cataloging-in-Publication Data is available at www.loc.gov or upon request from the publisher.

ISBN: 979-8-89232-875-3 (hardcover)
ISBN: 979-8-89232-961-3 (paperback)
ISBN: 979-8-89232-905-7 (ebook)

© 2025 BookLife Publishing
This edition is published by arrangement with BookLife Publishing.

North American adaptations © 2025 Bearport Publishing Company. All rights reserved. No part of this publication may be reproduced in whole or in part, stored in any retrieval system, or transmitted in any form or by any means, electronic, mechanical, photocopying, recording, or otherwise, without written permission from the publisher.

For more information, write to Bearport Publishing, 5357 Penn Avenue South, Minneapolis, MN 55419.

CONTENTS

Your Journey at Sea 4

Leif Erikson 6

Zheng He 10

Ferdinand Magellan 12

Jeanne Baret 16

Bungaree 18

Fabian Gottlieb von Bellingshausen 22

William Beebe 24

Dr. Sylvia Earle 26

Where Will a Journey at Sea Take You? . . . 30

Glossary 31

Index 32

Read More 32

Learn More Online 32

YOUR JOURNEY AT SEA

Ahoy! We are setting sail to follow some of the greatest pioneers at sea.

Most of our planet is covered by water. Many great explorers have traveled the oceans in the hopes of discovering something new.

Their journeys bring us to many places around the world. There is so much for us to see!

It is time to climb aboard and let the adventure begin!

LEIF ERIKSON

AROUND 970–1020

Our journey begins in Iceland, where a **Viking** named Leif Erikson was born.

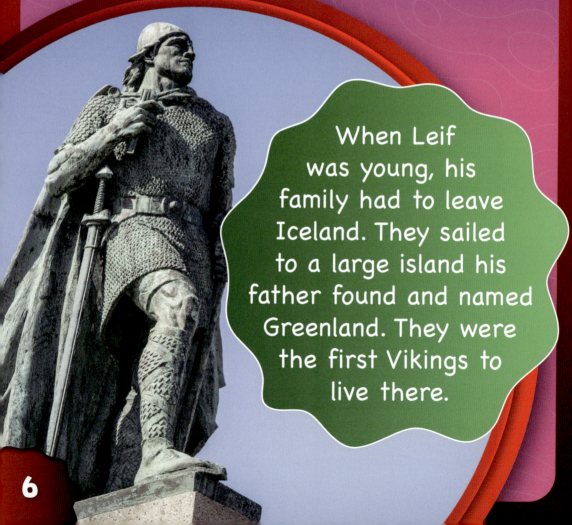

When Leif was young, his family had to leave Iceland. They sailed to a large island his father found and named Greenland. They were the first Vikings to live there.

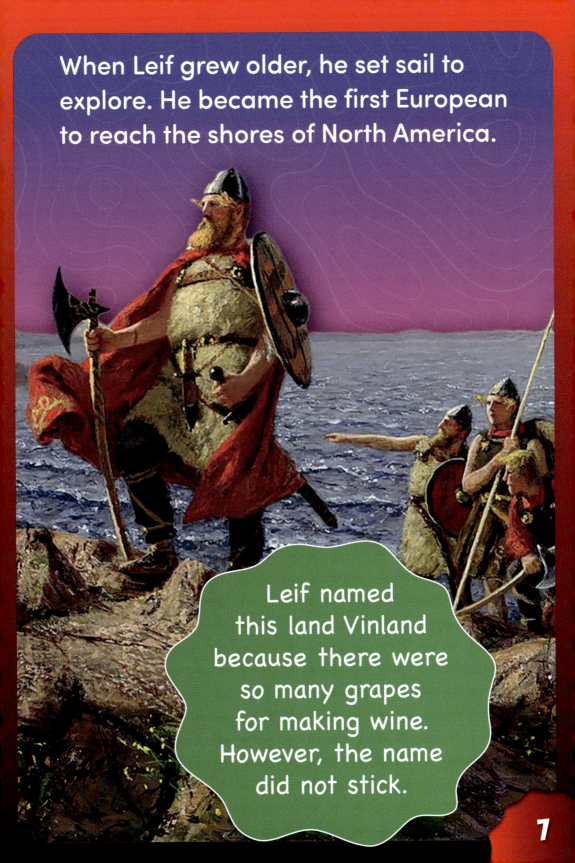

When Leif grew older, he set sail to explore. He became the first European to reach the shores of North America.

Leif named this land Vinland because there were so many grapes for making wine. However, the name did not stick.

On Leif's journey back to Greenland, he was said to have saved people whose ship was destroyed. This heroic act earned him the nickname Leif the Lucky.

Leif brought the people back to Greenland and helped them find homes.

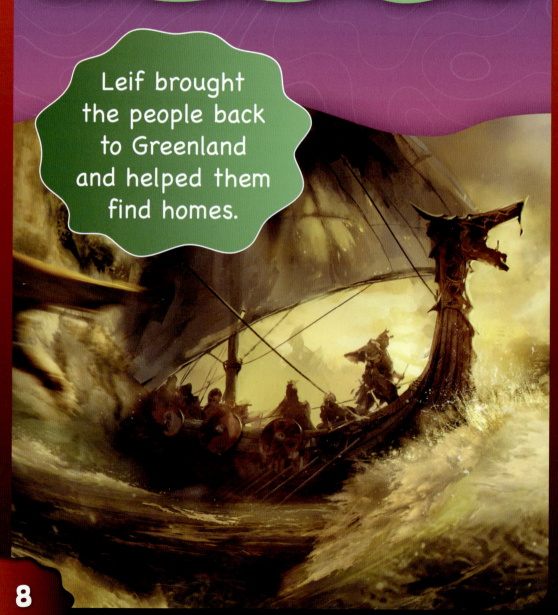

Now, we celebrate this explorer every October 9th with Leif Erikson Day.

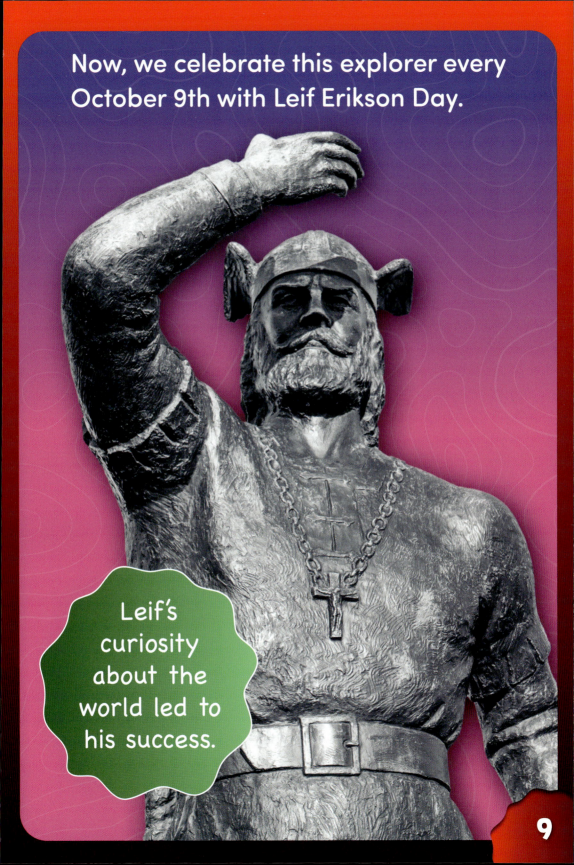

Leif's curiosity about the world led to his success.

ZHENG HE

AROUND 1371–1433

Here we are in China. This is where Zheng He was born.

Zheng He was in charge of the **emperor** of China's treasure ships. Zheng went on several journeys to show off China's wealth and power.

During his travels, Zheng was given many gifts to bring back to the emperor. Once, he brought back a giraffe! Some people thought it was a magical animal.

Zheng's adventures helped China trade with many other countries.

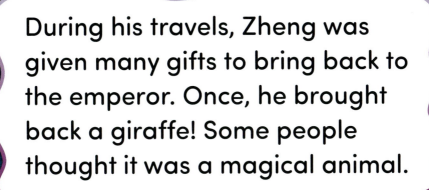

FERDINAND MAGELLAN

1480–1521

The next adventure is with Ferdinand Magellan!

When Ferdinand was born, no one had ever sailed around the world. He wanted to try to do it. Ferdinand was from Portugal, but he started his journey in Spain.

Ferdinand began sailing west, hoping to find a new path across the seas. He discovered a waterway at the bottom of South America. It allowed him to travel from the Atlantic Ocean to the Pacific Ocean.

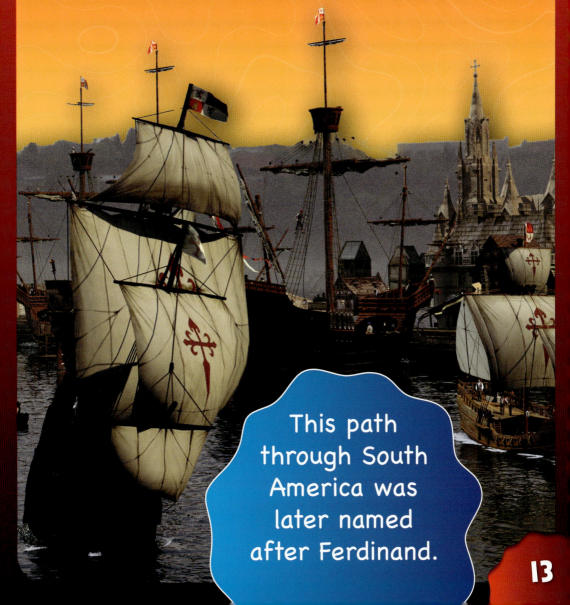

This path through South America was later named after Ferdinand.

After 99 days sailing the Pacific Ocean, Ferdinand and his crew finally found land. Sadly, the explorer died a few days later.

Ferdinand's **navigator**, Juan Sebastián Elcano, took over and completed the journey.

JUAN SEBASTIÁN ELCANO

Juan and the rest of the crew that made it were the first people to sail around the world in one trip.

Although Ferdinand did not complete the journey, he is remembered as a skilled leader.

JEANNE BARET

1740–1807

We are going around the world again! This time, let's learn how a French woman named Jeanne Baret made history.

Jeanne wanted to join a trip to sail around the world. At the time, however, women were not allowed to sail.

Jeanne **disguised** herself as a man and joined the trip. On the journey, she studied the many plants she saw. Now, there is even a flower named after her.

Jeanne's **determination** helped her become the first woman to sail around the world.

BUNGAREE

AROUND 1775–1830

Get ready to go Down Under! Our next stop is Australia. This is where Bungaree was born. He was an **Aboriginal** Australian.

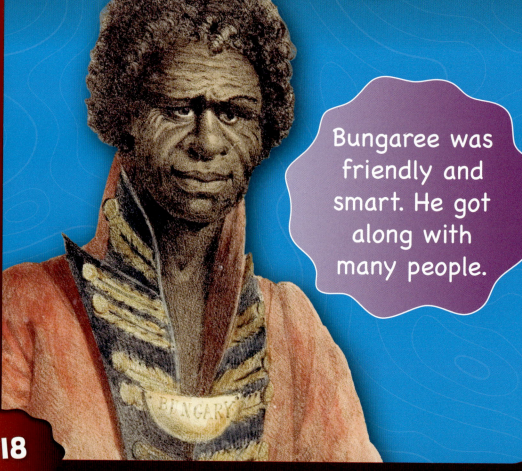

Bungaree was friendly and smart. He got along with many people.

Bungaree traveled with Matthew on a journey around Australia. He was the only person on the ship who was born in that country.

Bungaree was the first Australian to sail around all of Australia.

During the trip, Bungaree helped map the coastline of his home country.

Bungaree's kindness helped him make connections with many people. He is remembered as a great explorer.

FABIAN GOTTLIEB VON BELLINGSHAUSEN

1778–1852

It is time to head very far south. Fabian Gottlieb von Bellingshausen was a Russian captain who wanted to sail to Antarctica.

Many other people had tried to travel to Antarctica, but the trip was too difficult.

Fabian's adventure took more than two years. Even though there were bad storms, Fabian did not give up. He became the first person to see Antarctica's mainland.

Now, one of Antarctica's seas is named after Fabian.

WILLIAM BEEBE

1877–1962

Let's dive below the waves! American scientist William Beebe wanted to study sea animals in their underwater homes.

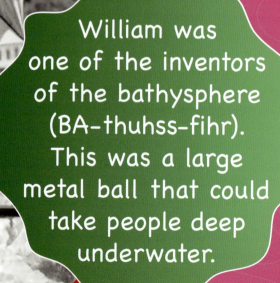

William was one of the inventors of the bathysphere (BA-thuhss-fihr). This was a large metal ball that could take people deep underwater.

Although the bathysphere was **dangerous**, William used it for more than 30 dives in the ocean.

During these underwater journeys, William discovered many deep-sea creatures that had never been seen before.

THE BATHYSPHERE

DR. SYLVIA EARLE

BORN 1935

Our last sea adventure is with Dr. Sylvia Earle. She is an American scientist who studies life in the ocean.

Sylvia has spent almost 7,000 hours underwater. During these journeys, she has set records and made many discoveries.

Early in her adventures, Sylvia became the first woman to dive down to 100 feet (30 m) in a deep-sea craft.

She also set the record for the deepest ocean walk, at about 1,250 ft. (380 m) below the surface.

Sylvia led an all-woman team who lived underwater for two weeks. They studied the effects of **pollution** on coral reefs.

She has made films and written books about her discoveries. Sylvia hopes that others will want to protect the oceans, too.

Sylvia also created an **organization** that works to protect ocean life from human harm.

DR. SYLVIA EARLE

Sylvia pushed herself to be her best. She has become one of the greatest divers on Earth.

WHERE WILL A JOURNEY AT SEA TAKE YOU?

Sailing around the world is exciting. And there is still so much of the sea to explore!

Would you like to lead the next journey at sea? One day, people may talk about your amazing adventures!

GLOSSARY

Aboriginal the first people to ever live in Australia

dangerous likely to cause harm

determination a strong will to do something

disguised dressed as someone else to fool others

emperor a person who rules over an area of land and its people

navigator a person who is trained to guide a ship from place to place

organization a group of people with a common interest or purpose

pollution substances that make the air, water, and land dirty

Viking a warrior from Norway, Denmark, or Sweden who lived from around 700 CE to about 1100 CE

31

INDEX

Aboriginal 18–19
Antarctica 22–23
bathysphere 24–25
dive 24–25, 27, 29
flower 17
maps 21
pollution 28
ships 8, 10, 19–20
treasure 10
Viking 6
world 5, 9, 12, 15–17, 30

READ MORE

Arbuthnott, Gill. *From Shore to Ocean Floor: The Human Journey to the Deep.* Somerville, MA: Big Picture Press, 2023.

Morey, Allan. *Exploring the Deep Sea (Dangerous Journeys).* Minneapolis: Bellwether Media, Inc., 2023.

LEARN MORE ONLINE

1. Go to **FactSurfer.com** or scan the QR code below.

2. Enter **"Pioneers at Sea"** into the search box.

3. Click on the cover of this book to see a list of websites.